Florida Panthers

Victoria Blakemore

For Ms. B, for your continued support and for always being

as excited about my books as I am!

Table of Contents

What Are Florida Panthers?

Florida panthers are large mammals. They are members of the puma family. They are closely related to pumas and cougars.

Although they are large cats, they are not part of the big cat family.

Florida panthers are tan in color

with a white belly.

Size

Florida panthers can range in length from six feet to eight feet long. They can weigh up to about 160 pounds.

Male panthers are usually larger than female panthers.

Physical Characteristics

Florida panthers are often mistaken for other large cats. The shape of their head and color of their fur is similar to other cats.

One way to tell them apart is their **crooked** tail. They also have a patch of fur on their back that grows in a different direction from the rest of their fur.

Florida panthers have good eyesight. Their **depth perception** is very good.

Habitat

Florida panthers are found in many different habitats. They can live in forests, prairies, and swamps.

They prefer areas with lots of plants so that they can hide and sneak up on their prey.

Range

Florida panthers are mainly found in south Florida.

They have also been seen in other

parts of Florida and Georgia.

Diet

Florida panthers are **carnivores**. They only eat meat.

Their diet is made up of white-tailed deer, hogs, rabbits, raccoons, and other small animals.

Florida panthers have a very good sense of smell. This helps them to find their prey.

Florida panthers do most of their hunting at night. This is because it is easier for them to sneak up on prey.

To catch their prey, they creep as close to it as they can. Then, they spring forward and catch it with their sharp claws.

Florida panthers are good **sprinters**. They do not usually chase prey for long distances.

Communication

Florida panthers use sound and smell to communicate with other panthers.

They have a special scent that they use to mark their **territory**. It lets other panthers know that the area is taken.

They can growl, purr, chirp, and scream. They cannot roar like some of the big cats.

Movement

Florida panthers can run at speeds up to thirty-five miles per hour. This is only for short distances.

They can travel long distances each day. Some have been known to travel over twenty miles in a day.

Florida panthers are good at climbing trees. They are also good swimmers.

Florida Panther Kittens

Florida panthers have a **litter** of between 1 and 4 babies. Their babies are called kittens.

They stay with their mother for up to two years. Their mother teaches them how to hunt.

Kittens are born with dark spots
that fade as they get older.

Florida Panther Life

Florida panthers are most active in the morning and evening. They prefer to rest in the middle of the day when it is hottest.

They are **solitary** animals. They spend most of their time alone.

Most Florida panthers are usually alone. This is not the case with mothers and kittens.

State Animal

Florida panthers are the official state animal of the state of Florida.

The Florida panther was chosen by students who voted in 1982. There were four choices: the Florida panther, alligator, manatee, and the key deer.

The Florida panther won the election with over 211,000 votes out of about 500,000.

Population

The Florida panther is one of the most **endangered** animals on Earth.

Researchers are not sure exactly how many are left in the wild. There are thought to be fewer than 150.

Florida panthers often live

between ten and fifteen years

in the wild.

Florida Panthers in Danger

Florida panthers face several main threats. Their habitats are being destroyed for farming and building.

They are often hit by cars as they cross roads that are being built through their habitats.

Florida panthers can also

become sick if they eat animals

that are high in **mercury**.

Helping Florida Panthers

The Florida Panther National Wildlife Refuge is an area of land where panthers are protected. It gives panthers a safe habitat to live in.

Signs are placed by roads where panthers have been seen. They warn drivers to watch for panthers crossing the road.

NEXT 2 MILES

Some Florida panthers that are born in **captivity** are being taught how to hunt. They are then released into the wild. This can help the population grow.

There is hope that through **conservation**, education, and release programs, the Florida panther will not become **extinct**.

Glossary

Captivity: animals that are kept by humans, not in the wild

Carnivore: an animal that eats only meat

Conservation: keeping something safe from loss or damage

Crooked: not straight

Depth Perception: the ability to judge distances between objects

Endangered: at risk of becoming extinct

Extinct: when there are no more of

an animal left in the wild

Litter: a group of animals born at the

same time

Mercury: a kind of metal

Solitary: living alone

Sprint: to run at top speed

Territory: an area of land that an

animal claims as its own

About the Author

Victoria Blakemore is a first grade

teacher in Southwest Florida with a

passion for reading.

You can visit her at

www.elementaryexplorers.com

Also in This Series

Gray Wolves — Sloths — Flamingos — Camels — Koalas — Honey Bees — Pandas

Pangolins — White-Tailed Deer — Orcas — Giraffes — Corn — Meerkats — Echidnas

Walruses — Raccoons — Bald Eagles — Apples — Arctic Foxes — Red Pandas — Cassowaries

Tigers — Ladybugs — Moose — Beluga Whales — Leopards — Elephants — Jellyfish

Binturongs — Lions — Dolphins — Reindeer — Hammerhead Sharks — Hippos — Pumpkins

Peafowl — Chameleons — Florida Panthers — Aye-Ayes — Black Bears — Cheetahs — Manatees

Gingerbread — Polar Bears — Hot Chocolate — Orangutans — Coyotes — Marshmallows — Strawberries

Also in This Series

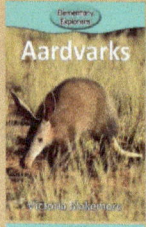

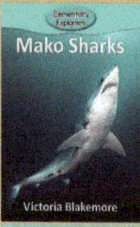

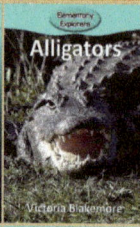

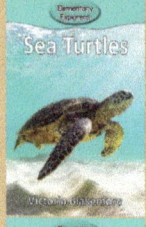

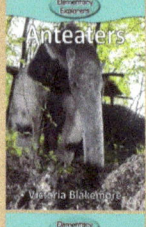

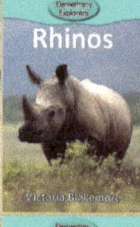

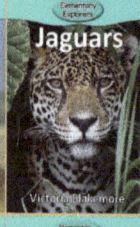

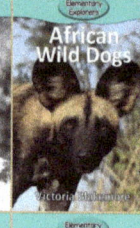

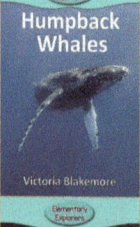

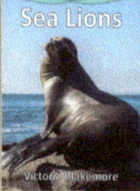

Aardvarks	Mako Sharks	Alligators	Frogs	Hedgehogs	Brown Bears	Bongos
Sea Turtles	Quokkas	Muskrats	Zebras	Red Foxes	Ring-Tailed Lemurs	Platypuses
Anteaters	Kangaroos	Rhinos	Jaguars	Wombats	Capybaras	Gorillas
Cats	Skunks	Butterflies	Dingoes	Snow Leopards	African Wild Dogs	Penguins
Whale Sharks	Wolverines	Warthogs	Caracals	Badgers	Seals	Hummingbird
Pikas	Humpback Whales	Pumas	Lemonade	Llamas	Tulips	Ostriches
Sunflowers	Fennec Foxes	Sea Lions	Squirrels	Roses	Porcupines	Ice Cream

Elementary Explorers

Victoria Blakemore

www.ingramcontent.com/pod-product-compliance
Lightning Source LLC
Chambersburg PA
CBHW051251020426
42333CB00025B/3160